£2.75

LOVE I

This book belongs to

LIZ.

LOVE POEMS

Yevgeny Yevtushenko

LONDON
VICTOR GOLLANCZ LTD
1977

First published in English in the U.S.A. under the title
From Desire to Desire
Copyright © 1976 by Doubleday & Company, Inc.

ISBN 0 575 02393 7 (Cloth)
ISBN 0 575 02397 X (Paper)

Printed in Great Britain by
Lowe & Brydone Printers Limited, Thetford, Norfolk

CONTENTS

A CONNOISSEUR OF LOVE KNOWS NOTHING OF LOVE

This is my second attempt at a foreword to this collection of love poetry. My editor dismissed my first effort with characteristic charm. "Not good enough, Genia," she said. Or, to give it its Russian translation, "Not good at *all*."

"Are you sure?" I asked with grim hopelessness. "Are you really sure a collection of love poetry should have a foreword?"

She readjusted her glasses and peered through them with the ruthless resolve of a horsebreaker on the wild prairies of publishing. "I m sure," she said.

And with that, she took off her glasses and, instantly, her face seemed embarrassed and vulnerable. "A woman with glasses is two women," I thought.

As always, I was disarmed by a woman's vulnerability. A

foreword about love? Unthinkable. Impossible. Love itself is a foreword!

One day when I was nine, my mother warned me as she was going out the door, "This bookcase is for children, and that one is for grownups. I've locked that one. Keep it locked—or else." Naturally, the first thing I did was grab a butter knife and, with its supple blade, jimmy open the forbidden bookcase. And so, at the tender age of nine, my favorite author became Maupassant, and I proceeded to devour all the shady love intrigues of Georges du Roy, that elegant cad who jimmied open the doors of high society with the waxed tips of his curled mustache. I didn't realize it at the time, but Georges was an unhappy man, totally denied his fair share of the gift of love. A connoisseur of love knows nothing of love.

I was driven not so much by a craving for love as a curiosity about it—and a covert one at that. There was something shameful, something rather damp and dirty about it. The sharper the attraction a young girl exercised over me, the greater my desire to yank her braids, as if to mask desire with disdain. The young girls were as inexperienced as I was, and soon I felt an even greater attraction to mature women, who seemed touched and enhanced by the magic of the Unknown. However intense the feeling, though, it was curiosity and not yet love.

*

The flesh is a dilettante; the soul, a seeker. The soul recoils from the interests of the flesh. The pursuit of one interferes with the pursuit of the other, and if the instinctive appetites of the flesh aren't curbed, the flesh can even turn and devour the soul. Only when soul and flesh understand one another can desire and love be chaste and clean.

Who among us hasn't had the following experience: You come home late at night, full of loathing for the world and for yourself—a feeling Blok captured perfectly in the lines:

> Meeting with a passerby
> You turn to spit into his face
> And stop—only because you spy
> The same desire in his eye.

Suddenly you see two young shadows in an embrace so pure you'd think there wasn't a drop of cynicism, lust, blood, or filth in the world. Indeed, if the whole world harbors only two such souls, we don't have the right to lose faith in the possibility of love.

*

Not so long ago, I ran into a poet on the street. His daily routine, to use his words, ran like this: "Up at seven; forty-five minutes with the dumbbells and a spongebath with cold water. Then a light, nutritious breakfast—fresh orange juice, grated carrots—and a look at the papers. (Fifteen minutes in all for that.) From eight to twelve, creation. I read once that Hemingway did all his writing standing up. I've put my typewriter on a stool and the stool on a table. It helps. At twelve, I switch off my consciousness. An hour-long walk before lunch." I ran into him during the sacred moment of his stroll, that moment of switched-off consciousness, which I strongly suspect never gets switched back on when he returns to his desk. He was striding along, majestically pounding his boots into the pavement when, wonder of wonders, he noticed me. "It happened!" he proclaimed in the hoarse whisper of a Tantalus who'd caught his prize. "What happened?" I asked with some apprehension. "I've finished my cycle! A hundred sonnets on love. I've covered the whole subject!"

There's a lucky man for you!

*

Why are true love and tragedy shackled to one another like two convicts on a chain? Because love is the perfection that the imperfection of the world enviously tries to stifle.

*

Pushkin had the ideal attitude toward women:

> I loved you once, I swear, so tenderly,
> As may God grant another hold you dear.

Not a trace of possessiveness. In Pushkin's love poetry the untamed charm of sensuality lives side by side with the embarrassed charm of restraint.

Someday someone will write a great new tragedy about the Romeo and Juliet of the West and East, against the backdrop of the cold war waged by our contemporary Montagues and Capulets.

*

In the love of a man for a woman and of a woman for a man lies the very root of Christianity: an attempt to conquer death. A child is the joint victory of a man and a woman over their own impermanence.

Love and art are alike; they alone can conquer death.

*

Russian seems to be the only language in which you can refer to a loved one as "my native one"—a phrase reserved in other languages for the place where you were born. But, then, love *is* the very place where we are born.

To this very day, people in the northern Russian countryside use the old-fashioned term "I take pity on you" to mean "I love you." Someone cooked up the absurd theory that pity degrades a person. Pity degrades only those who don't know how to pity others.

*

The other day, I ran into a scoundrel of the lowest order—ears like a bat's, a face as pale as death, bursting with the complacency of someone who'd just pulled off a dirty trick on someone else. There are a lot of nasty rumors going round about him. Fact is, he's the embodiment of a nasty rumor about himself. His face almost always expresses a readiness to do something vile—sweet little venemous eyes, thin lips, almost invisible, but always moist with anticipation. They have a phrase for people like that. "Hyenas in syrup," they call them. How could anyone want to crawl into the same bed with something like that? And yet they do, they do.

There are plenty of incorrigible men—some so "rhinocerized" that, to borrow Ionesco's expression, a single flower couldn't grow on them. And then, there are women fallen so low they can't fall any further, who, like the earth itself, burst into bloom at the first tender touch.

*

Pasternak once wrote, "All life long love draws away; love, the evanescent gift of wonder." Really, though, is love so momentary? You can strip a man of everything, you can throw him naked and cold onto the floor of a solitary cell, but who can tear the memory of his best moments from beneath his flesh? Moments don't shrink, they expand in time, like Balzac's wrong-sided shagreen leather.

*

It's not envy I feel but a kind of pity and revulsion for men who try always to be seen in the company of beautiful women. There is a certain spiritual inferiority in that, a hunger for self-affirmation: "Look at me! I've got a beautiful new woman by my side. I'm worth something!"

A tall woman with dazzling white skin passed by. She looked like the Vénus de Milo with severed arms restored. It hurt to look at her, that's how beautiful she was. She sat down and started to eat. And suddenly, in the way she held her fork, in her small, predatory movements, in her tittering, there was an expression of such homeliness she couldn't have looked worse if her arms had fallen off again, taking her head with them. The woman sitting next to her, who but a moment before had seemed so unattractive in comparison, smiled so softly you'd have thought all the lost beauty of the world had been resurrected in her. Wasn't that the reason Zabolotsky asked:

> And if that's true, then what is beauty,
> And why is it idolized?
> Is it a vessel, void and empty,
> Or is it the fire that burns inside?

*

Once, long ago, I was walking alone down Gorky Street through the falling snow at three in the morning. Suddenly I stopped. From out of the snowstorm, Pasternak came toward me. He had his arm around a blue-eyed woman in a downy white shawl, her cheeks flushed with happiness and the wind. Apparently she had just returned from someplace far away, and he ran beside and a little ahead of her to see her better and to kiss away the snowflakes from her face. He was laughing like a child. He was then, if I'm not mistaken, sixty-five years old.

*

Some people adopt a rather conspiratorial attitude toward love poetry. To them, the lyrics are mere raw material for scandal about the private life of the author. When I first published one of the poems in this collection, "I Fell Out of Love with You," absolute strangers called up my wife and raged, "He's shamed you before the entire country!" When I wrote the poem "Masha," a respected older poet claimed I had compromised not only Masha, poor child, but her mother—an honest writer—as well. The brother of the heroine of the title poem of this book, "From Desire to Desire," took a more noble attitude. After an evening in which I'd read aloud that poem with some others, I asked him, glancing with some trepidation at his strong, young biceps, which poem was his favorite. "Unfortunately," he replied with a smile, "the one dedicated to my sister."

*

If ever you find people looking at you with arrogance or with something base and obscene in their eyes, stop and consider: Have they ever loved? And while you're at it, ask yourself: "Have I?"

*

A husband who worshiped his wife, once whispered conspiratorially in my ear, "Do you know when she and I get the greatest pleasure?" "No, when?" I asked, expecting at long last some insight into what had always been the mysterious marvel of their love. "When we're completely alone and we take the phone off the hook, lock the door, and eat garlic!" Lucky man!

*

I have nothing but contempt for couples who use their own happiness to fence out the unhappiness of the rest of the world. It's little more than a conspiracy of two against mankind. The only people who can be absolutely happy are absolute idiots.

*

He was forty-three, she was forty-nine. They had known each other for quite a while, but now they were together for the first time.

"I've always had men who were older than you," she said. "You're my youngest lover."

Youngest lover! When she was eighteen, her first man had been twenty, and yet that man now seemed older to her than the forty-three-year-old man who lay beside her and thought that his life was done.

—Yevgeny Yevtushenko

Moscow, 1976

TRANSLATED BY ANTHONY KAHN

LOVE POEMS

SLEEP, MY BELOVED . . .

The salty spray glistens on the fence.
The wicket gate is bolted tight.
                        And the sea,
smoking and heaving and scooping the dikes,
has sucked into itself the salty sun.
Sleep, my beloved . . .
                        don't torment my soul.
Already the mountains and the steppe are falling asleep,
and our lame dog,
                        shaggy and sleepy,
lies down and licks his salty chain.
And the branches are murmuring
                        and the waves are trampling
and the dog and his day
                        are on the chain,
and I say to you whispering
                        and then half whispering
and then quite silently,
                        "Sleep, my beloved . . ."
Sleep, my beloved . . .
                        Forget that we quarreled.
Imagine—
        we are waking.
                        Everything is new.
We are lying in the hay,
                        We sleepyheads.

Part of the dream
is the scent of sour cream, from somewhere below, from
   the cellar.
Oh how can I make you
                    imagine all this,
you, so mistrustful?
                    Sleep, my beloved . . .
Smile in your dream.
                    Put away your tears.
Go and gather flowers
                    and wonder where to put them,
burying your face in them.
Are you muttering?
                    Tired, perhaps, of tossing?
Muffle yourself up in your dream
                    and wrap yourself in it.
In your dream you can do whatever you want to,
all that we mutter about
                    if we don't sleep.
It's reckless not to sleep,
                    it's even a crime.
All that is latent
                    cries out from the depths.
It is difficult for your eyes.
                    So much crowded into them.
It will be easier for them under closed eyelids.
Sleep, my beloved . . .
                    What is it that's making you sleepless?
Is it the roaring sea?
                    The begging of the trees?
Evil forebodings?
                    Someone's dishonesty?

And maybe, not someone's,
                              but simply my own?
Sleep, my beloved . . .
                    Nothing can be done about it.
But no, I am innocent of that accusation.
Forgive me—do you hear!
                    Love me—do you hear!
Even if in your dream!
                    Even if in your dream!
Sleep, my beloved . . .
                    We are on the earth,
flying savagely along,
                    threatening to explode,
and we have to embrace
                    so we won't fall down,
and if we do fall—
                    we shall fall together.
Sleep, my beloved . . .
                    don't nurse a grudge.
Let dreams settle softly in your eyes.
It's so difficult to fall asleep on this earth!
And yet—
          Do you hear, beloved?—
                    Sleep.
And the branches are murmuring
                    and the waves are trampling
and the dog and his day
                    are on the chain,
and I say to you, whispering
                    and then half whispering

and then quite silently,

              "Sleep, my beloved . . ."

TRANSLATED BY GEOFFREY DUTTON WITH
TINA TUPIKINA-GLAESSNER

THE CITY OF YES AND
THE CITY OF NO

I am like a train
            rushing for many years now
between the city of Yes
            and the city of No.
My nerves are strained
            like wires
between the city of No
            and the city of Yes.

Everything is deadly,
            everyone frightened, in the city of No.
It's like a study furnished with dejection.
In it every object is frowning, withholding something,
and every portrait looks out suspiciously.
Every morning its parquet floors are polished with bile,
its sofas are made of falsehood, its walls of misfortune.
You'll get lots of good advice in it—like hell you will!—
not a bunch of flowers, or even a greeting.
Typewriters are chattering a carbon-copy answer:
"No—no—no . . . No—no—no. No—no—no."
And when the lights go out altogether,
the ghosts in it begin their gloomy ballet.
You'll get a ticket to leave—like hell you will!—
to leave the black town of No.

But in the town of Yes—
                    life's like the song of a thrush.
This town's without walls—
                    just like a nest.
The sky is asking you to take any star
                    you like in your hand.
Lips ask for yours, without any shame,
softly murmuring:
                    "Ah—all that nonsense!"
And in no one is there even a trace of suspicion,
and lowing herds are offering their milk,
and daisies, teasing, are asking to be picked,
and wherever you want to be, you are instantly there,
taking any train, or plane, or ship that you like.
And water, faintly murmuring, whispers through the years:
"Yes—yes—yes. Yes—yes—yes. Yes—yes—yes."
To tell the truth, the snag is it's a bit boring at times,
to be given so much, almost without any effort,
in that shining multicolored city of Yes.

Better let me be tossed around—
                    to the end of my days,
between the city of Yes
                    and the city of No!
Let my nerves be strained
                    like wires
between the city of No
                    and the city of Yes!

TRANSLATED BY GEOFFREY DUTTON WITH
TINA TUPIKINA-GLAESSNER

EARLY ILLUSIONS

Early illusions are beautiful,
Early illusions are wounding
But what does it matter! We are above vanity,
we embrace the highest knowledge,
saved by our happy blindness.

We, who are not afraid of taking a false step—
fools, from the common point of view—
still keep enchantment in our faces
through all the disillusioned crowd.

We are driven towards the distance
                    by a glimmering of something,
away from the daily grind, the calculations of everyday
    living,
from pale skeptics and pink schemers,
transforming the world with our reflections.

But the inevitability of disappointments
makes us see too clearly . . . On all sides
everything suddenly takes shape,
all unknown to us till now.

The world appears before us, unhazed; unmisted,
no longer radiant with something priceless,
but with all this truthfulness unmasked
as deceit. But what is gone—
                    was no deception.

You see, it is not the knowledge of the serpent,
it is not the doubtful honor of experience,
but the ability to be enchanted by the world
that reveals to us the world as it really is.

Suppose someone with illusions in his eyes
flashes past, pursuing some distant gleam,
then it doesn't seem to us that he is blind—
it seems to us that we ourselves are blind.

TRANSLATED BY GEOFFREY DUTTON WITH
TINA TUPIKINA-GLAESSNER

THE INCENDIARY

You are completely free of affectation:
silent you sit, watchfully tense,
just as silence itself pretends to nothing
on a starless night in a fire-gutted city.

Consider that city—it is your past,
wherein you scarcely ever managed to laugh,
now raging through the streets, now sunk in self,
between your insurrections and your calms.

You wanted life and gave it all your strength,
but, sullenly spurning everything alive,
this slum of a city suffocated you
with the dreary weight of its architecture.

In it every house was shuttered tight,
in it shrewdness and cynicism ruled,
it never hid its poverty of spirit,
its hate for anyone who wasn't broken.

And so one night you burned it down
and ran for cover, frightened by the flames,
till chance produced me in your way, the one
you stumbled on when you were fugitive.

I took you in my arms, I felt you tremble,
as quietly your body clung to mine,
not knowing me or caring, but yet,
like an animal, grateful for my pity.

Together then we sallied . . . where did we go?
Wherever our eyes, in their folly, took us.
But intermittently you had to turn
to watch your past ominously burning.

It burned beyond control, till it was ashes.
And I remain tormented to this day
that you are drawn, as though enchanted,
back to that place where still the embers glow.

You're here with me, and yet not here.
In fact you have abandoned me. You glide
through the smoldering wreckage of the past,
holding aloft a bluish light in your hand.

What pulls you back? It's empty and gray there!
Oh the mysterious power of the past!
You never could learn to love it as it was,
but yet you fell madly in love with its ruins.

Ashes and embers must be magnets too.
How can we tell what potencies they hold?
Over what's left where once she set her fire
the incendiary cries like a little child.

TRANSLATED BY STANLEY KUNITZ
WITH ANTHONY KAHN

DAMP WHITE IMPRINTS

Damp white imprints dog the feet;
snowbound trolley; snowbound street.
Her tip of glove to lip and cheek,
"Good-by." Go.
Deathly, into soaring snow
and stillness, as expected, go.
A turn:
       the plunge to the metro.
A blare of lights. A melting hat.
I stand, am spun in drafts, see black,
take the tunnel, train, and track,
sit and wait as others sat,
touch cold marble, chill my hand
and, heavyhearted, understand
that nothing ever really happened,
ever would, ever can.

1956

TRANSLATED BY ANTHONY KAHN

MASHA

A girl goes along the seashore
blushing and shy
a tide rising in her
a woman rising in her

She takes off her shoes by the sea
and steps into it as into music
And she understands everything
though she doesn't understand a thing

Reason and rashness mixed—
A keen glance through us
and then again withdrawn—
All this is Masha—
a serious wide-eyed being

And the roof of my mouth goes dry
when her slender boyish legs
heedless of some grownup's opinion
bear her helplessly to me

And on the wet sand by an old boat
with growing confidence I kiss
all that Masha's arms are—from elbow
to the rose petals of her nails

I put on my snorkel gear
and Masha swims somewhere above me
I search for Masha through the glass
as if drunk among the crabs and flowers

And I see in the bright green gloaming
in a bank of clouds above the underwater ridge
her legs like white stalks
fluttering submerged

And I swim and swim in the underwater thickets
and I swim, my fins thatching the water,
and I'm unhappy because I'm happy
and then happy because I'm unhappy

What can I say? Tell Mother not to worry
Masha I'll do you no harm
Masha I ask so little of you
and yet so much—just that you exist—

In meditations on death and eternity
gripped by hope and melancholy
I look through your slender little heart
as through a transparent pebble in the sea

1958

TRANSLATED BY LAWRENCE FERLINGHETTI
WITH ANTHONY KAHN

IRENE

How do you do, Irene?
How are you, Irene?
Without phoning
I came again,
for I know
you'll forgive me for this,
you won't send me away again,
but will take me in and give me something to eat,
and will share my sorrows.
I am neither your husband nor your lover,
not even taking off my coat
I hold your hand carefully
between mine,
and kiss you on the forehead
while you blush.
You would make such a charming wife—
devoted,
loyal,
responsive.
And my friends would laugh:
"How could you, Genia!"

Oh think!—
Who will
marry her?
How many men has she had in her life—but not one lasted.

Is it possible that she, of all people, could still fall in love?
Because you are
                    so kind,
every brute made use of you.
My dearest,
            how
                    you were deceived!
How
        you were blemished
                            and stained!
And yet your soul—
                    is so girlish!
Here you sit,
        shining with goodness,
all shy and childlike.
How could it be
                that now you have
someone to sleep with
                but no one to wake up with?

Once, your brown eyes
                were clear,
now your brown eyes are sad,
but they remain beautiful,
pure and kind,
            Russian.
May you meet someone the same,
shining with the same goodness!
May you keep safe not your childish virginity
but the great virginity
                    of womanhood.

May you be spared from merciless anguish,
my dearest one,
    tender,
        unfortunate . . .

TRANSLATED BY GEOFFREY DUTTON WITH
TINA TUPIKINA-GLAESSNER

STOLEN APPLES

Fences careened in the storm;
we stole through the bitter shadows
like thieving children warmed
by shirtfuls of stolen apples.

The apples wanted to spill;
to bite them was scandalous.
But we loved one another
and that fact redeemed us.

Secluding the criminal twins
in a cosmos of dirty waves,
the snug cottage whispered,
"Be brave and love . . . be brave . . ."

The cottage's owner, an ex-
soccer hero, from his photo
dim on the glimmering mantel,
urged, "Be bold . . . plunge through . . ."

So, pivoting and twisting,
we burst through the penalty zone,
slipped past the last defender,
and billowed the nets of the goal!

Rest period. Above us, dust
flickered; we seemed to dream,
small soccer shoes vibrated
on an invisible field.

"Play," each mote insisted,
"Play, but play earnestly.
The earth's heavy globe is a speck
Like us, essentially."

We played again; we kicked.
The game perhaps was stupid
but we did love one another
and that felt splendid.

Drugged by its roaring, the sea
mumbled of something profound
but then a golden fish, your bang,
splashed upon your brow,

and I was unconcerned to know
that once on the storm's other side,
for all my bravura folly,
I'd sink back with the tide.

Let slander pursue me;
love isn't for the feeble.
The odor of love is the scent
not of bought but of stolen apples.

What matters the watchman's shout
when, wrapped in the sea's far hiss,
I can cushion my head between
two salty apples I've filched.

TRANSLATED BY JOHN UPDIKE
WITH ANTHONY KAHN

I DREAMED I ALREADY LOVED YOU

I dreamed I already loved you.
I dreamed I already killed you.

But you rose again; another form, but you,
A girl on the little ball of the earth,
Naïve simplicity, curve-necked
On that early canvas of Picasso,
And prayed to me with your ribs,
"Love me," as though you said, "Don't push me off."

I'm that played-out, grown-up acrobat,
Hunchbacked with senseless muscles,
Who knows that advice is a lie,
That sooner or later there's falling.

I'm too scared to say I love you,
Because I'd be saying I'll kill you.

For in the depths of a face I can see through
I see the faces—can't count them—
Which, right on the spot, or maybe
Not right away, I tortured to death.

You're pale from the mortal balance. You say,
"I know everything; I was all of them.
I know you've already loved me.
I know you've already killed me.

But I won't spin the globe backwards
We're on: Love again, and then kill again."

Lord, you're young. Stop your globe.
I'm tired of killing. I'm not a damn thing but old.

You move the earth beneath your little feet,
You fall, "Love me."
It's only in those eyes—so similar, you say,
"This time don't kill me."

TRANSLATED BY JAMES DICKEY
WITH ANTHONY KAHN

THE OLD HOUSE

The old house was swaying, composing a chorale with its
creaking,
and the creaking of the chorale was a funeral service sung
for us.
This house of many creaks could sense that secretly
you and I were slowly mingling with its dust.

"Do not die yet"—the words were in the neighing from the
meadows,
in the long howl of the dogs, the incantation of the pines,
but side by side, each to the other, we were dying already,
and that is the same as is generally known as dying.

And yet what a yearning to live! The woodpecker tapping
the pinelog,
a tame hedgehog running about in the mushrooms near the
house,
and the night floating like a shaggy-coated, wet, black dog,
holding a star like a water lily in its mouth.

Through the window the darkness was breathing the scent
of wet raspberries,
and behind my back—my back had eyes that never
missed!—
my beloved was sleeping with Platonov's *Fro*,* worn out
with worries,
as peacefully as with a newly discovered sister.

* A novel by the modern Russian writer Platonov (1899–1951). His
story *Fro* (first published in 1936) depicts a woman in love.

I lay thinking of the dull imperfection of marriages,
of the dishonorableness of us all—traitors, dissemblers.
For I loved you as much as forty thousand brother-warriors,
and was destroying you as if they all were enemies.

What good thing then has all my fiery declaiming stirred,
if, scattering myself from the stage, making the clichés roll,
I wanted to give happiness to the whole world
and found I could not give it to one living soul?

Yes, you're a different person now. The tightening of your
                                                    eyelids
is angry and merciless. Bitter your ridicule of other people.
And yet, who but we ourselves make those we love
into such creatures, loving them is beyond our power?

Yes, we were dying. But there was something that would
                                                 not let me
be completely convinced that you and I did not exist.
Love still existed there. Love could still draw breath
and mist the mirror held in front of her weak lips.

Swaying and creaking amongst the nettles, the old house
                                                  survived,
volunteering to lend us its endurance.
We were dying in it, but we were still alive.
We loved each other, this was the proof of our existence.

Sometime in the future—God do not let me, do not let me!
when I will fall out of love with you, and really die,
my flesh will stir in the darkness and secretly laugh at me:
"You're alive!"—it will whisper in the deceptive fever of the
                                                      night.

But in the drive of passion, wiser, though sadly mortified,
suddenly I will understand that the voice of the flesh tells
lies,
and I will say to myself: "I fell out of love. I died.
But once upon a time I loved and was alive."

TRANSLATED BY GEOFFREY DUTTON
WITH IGOR MEZHAKOFF-KORIAKIN

GLASHA, BRIDE OF THE OCEAN
(A *Tale of the North Country*)

She knows the river, net and hook,
and hunts it deep as any.
Love opens her a petaled look:
"I couldn't care a penny!
You're better dead!"
She shakes her head,
her angry earrings dance.
She walks in scarfs and sarafans
she spins from Northern Light!
No other finger trains her hair
or teaches tress to toss and play,
no other ribbon winds her braid
than the river's wave!
She moves along the shore
and mends her nets. She beams
a leaping look beneath her brow
as salmon scale a stream!
I stood enchanted at the root
and dared a timid dream of fruit.
But tongues did roll in pub and spire
and toss about her name
and bandy it in crew and choir
and gossip she was tamed.
Oh! I cried,
"Who bends the wind? Who drowns the rain?"

Mad I walked.
             "It's all a joke!"
The townsmen puffed their pipes and spoke
me silent smoke.
"Who rings her finger? Who braids her hair?"
I faced Northwest
and asked the air.

Suddenly up by my side
pops a tramp,
sprouting like a tundra toadstool
in the damp.
"Give a drink and get an answer;
by and by," says he,
"I'll shed a secret on your saucer
like a sprig of tea."
He drains a glass and drains another
and drinks my money dry.
Then:
"The icy ocean is her lover,"
he winks,
"And she's his bride."

I stood up fierce, my stormy fists
raged to pound his frame.
"They make a plaything of my pain
for fowl and fish to see;
the deep pike cackles in the river,
the high loon howls at me!"

Glasha busies at her boat,
tarring back and side,

and shows the sun her mended sail
stitched to leak no light.
I speak my heart:
                    "Above the wave
the fish leaps and the dipping drake
skims a hungry beak.
For your velvet look I'd lay
the tundra at your feet
and lullaby your tattered coat
to sleep in ermine sheets,
and track the fishes' mating steps
from deepest sea to spawning pool
and catch a salmon in my net
rich with roe of pearls,
and trap you dreams you never dared
and what you wished of wildest fruit
to slake the travels of your boots
through salty sea and scale.
You tricked my lip upon your hook
and lure of flashing teeth,
and now I'm bluffed of coin and keep
and townsmen tell me, drunk and brief,
you're promised to the sea!"

Answers Glasha,
                    "I'm his bride.
Look at the river. Restless water
runs beneath the wave
and hastens to the grayer fathoms
where my lover waits. Today
I'll lift an oar and lure a breeze
to sail me, unannounced, to sea.

I'll drop beneath the cloudy night
and hug the thunder of his breast
till all is dark forgetfulness
and dreams of things that come and go
upon the sighing of a pillow
made of porpoises at rest.
I'll ask my age, I'll hear him say
that all my turns about the sun
were seventeen salmon in a wave
and seventeen fish scales on a blade.
In rolling thunder
and chilly light
he'll rumble me his answers
and speak to me of life.
Lad, your words won't win a wife
for all they'll ever say of life
when I have heard the sea!"

Her ship gained snowy sail at that,
cupped a breeze,
and drew her on a sharp tack
to the sea.
I whispered words I soon forgot
and turned with empty eyes from what
I might have had of life, but for the sea.
And felt the fact drop like a hook
that caught and drew a moan from me,
"What will I ever say of life
to ears that heard the sea?"

TRANSLATED BY ANTHONY KAHN

A SUPERFLUOUS MIRACLE

Everything, for heaven's sake, would have been simpler,
and probably kinder and wiser,
if I hadn't rushed to accept a gift
without giving it a thought.

And in the darkness, all my senses aware,
out of those shed clothes was born
this white superfluous miracle
in a dark cloud of sinful hair.

And when I stepped out into the street
I was not expecting what I found—
I heard only snow above me,
I saw only snow beneath me.

The city looked strict, fit for skis,
and the mud hid itself under the snowdrifts,
and the leaning, shrouded cranes
flew motionlessly through the snow.

What for, where from, why?—
by what kind of foolish love
was this new superfluous miracle
suddenly dumped on my shoulders?

Life, it would be better to strike me,
to chop me up for firewood,
than endow me so senselessly—
those gifts are a burden.

You are kind, you can't be faulted,
but there is evil in your tenderheartedness.
If you weren't so beautiful
you wouldn't also be so terrible.

And that god who cries from hidden places
somewhere deep inside me,
is he also (no doubt) a superfluous miracle?
Without him I would be more peaceful . . .

Thus I wandered and wandered along the white deserted
    footpath,
tormenting myself, tormenting someone else,
crushed by the gift of beauty
that mowed me down . . .

TRANSLATED BY GEOFFREY DUTTON WITH
TINA TUPIKINA-GLAESSNER

SECRET MYSTERIES

Adolescent mysteries melt away
like mist upon the shore
The Tonyas and Tanyas were all mysteries
even with cold sores on their legs

Stars and animals were mysteries
Mushrooms under aspen trees
and doors creaking mysteriously—
only in childhood do doors creak that way

The world's riddles rose up
like balloons from the mouth
of some seductive fakir
full of crafty schemes

Enchanted snowflakes
fell in fields and woods
Enchanted laughter
danced in young girls' eyes

Mysteriously we whispered something
on the mysterious ice of a skating rink
mystery touching mystery
hand touching hand

Unexpectedly maturity caught up with us
His dress coat worn to holes
the fakir went on tour
in someone else's childhood

We grownups forgotten
Ah, fakir, you're a faker!
So unmysterious it hurts
snow falls on our shoulders

Where are you, bewitched balloons?
There's no mystery to our mourning
Others are unmysterious to us
and we're unmysterious to them

And if some hand by chance
caress us lightly
it still is only a hand and not a mystery
a hand, understand, only a hand

Oh give me a mystery, some simple mystery
a secret mystery—silence and timidity—
a fragile mystery, a barefoot mystery—
just one sweet secret mystery!

1960

TRANSLATED BY LAWRENCE FERLINGHETTI
WITH ANTHONY KAHN

A GIRL WAS PLAYING
THE ACCORDION

A girl was playing the accordion,
the wine was in her head,
and garlic made the blunt end glisten
on a loaf of bread.

It took no breach of blood or brass
to raise a banquet in a shack;
geologists in arms we were
who caught her song and sang it back.

I knew a girl who knew the land;
I sat beside her steady chair
and felt her unfamiliar hand
ride my rustling hair.

I sort of drank, I sort of didn't,
and mined the levels of my pain;
I sort of wasn't her beloved
and her beloved all the same.

The other girl pushed and pulled
a song of seas and distant shores,
and as she sang her rubber boots
slapped her legs and sores.

She sang of lonely, burning days,
an ache at heart, an ash of grief,
of limitless and faraway
fences, fires, trees.

The girl sang on and always on
while her sister, schooled in dust and stones,
wept until the quiet dawn
the tears of old, forgotten bones.

TRANSLATED BY ANTHONY KAHN

COLORS

When your face
appeared over my crumpled life
at first I understood
only the poverty of what I have.
Then its particular light
on woods, on rivers, on the sea,
became my beginning in the colored world
in which I had not yet had my beginning.
I am so frightened, I am so frightened,
of the unexpected sunrise finishing,
of revelations
and tears and the excitement finishing.
I don't fight it, my love is this fear,
I nourish it who can nourish nothing,
love's slipshod watchman.
Fear hems me in.
I am conscious that these minutes are short
and that the colors in my eyes will vanish
when your face sets.

TRANSLATED BY HERBERT MARSHALL

DEEP SNOW

I am skiing over the white snow.
Skiing fast, I ask:
                    "What can I do in life?"
I peer into myself,
                strain,
                    remember.
What do I know?
                    I know nothing.
I am skiing over the white snow.
There's Nogin Square in the handsome town.
I can spy the square from where I am.
A girl I know lives there.
                        She
is no wife to me.
                    Nor is she in love.
Who is to blame? . . .
                        Ah, the white spume.
I am skiing fast.
                    I feel troubled and light.
The snow is deep.
                    And deep my breathing.
Overhead it's also deep.
It's a long way I have to go . . .
Creak on,
        dear skis,
                    creak on,
and you,
        far away,
                forget your distress.

Screw up your courage.
                    Go out and shop.
Sleep soundly.
                I'll not get lost.
I feel like smoking,
                break some matches.
I'm weary of running from myself.
I'll ride home instead.
                    In a hot electric train
my skis will jab some passenger.
Then I'll arrive and visit a girl.
                        She'll stop what she is doing.
She wears thick plaits in a garland.
She yearned for me from afar.
She will ask to be kissed.
"Did you have trouble with the skis?"
                            She'll softly ask.
"No, no," I'll answer.
                "No trouble at all" . . .
And I'll begin to think.
                "A cup of tea, my dear?"
"No."
    "What's the matter?
                    I don't understand. . . .
Where are you now?"
                I shake my head.
What shall I answer?
                And I reply:
"I am skiing over the white snow."

1955

TRANSLATED BY GEORGE REAVY

I HUNG A POEM ON A BRANCH

I hung a poem
                on a branch.
Thrashing,
            it resists the wind.
"Take it down,
            don't joke,"
                            you urge.
People pass.
            Stare in surprise.
Here's a tree
            waving
                a poem.
Don't argue now.
                We have to go on.
"You don't know it by heart!" . . .
                            "That's true,
but I'll write a fresh poem for you tomorrow."
It's not worth being upset by such trifles!
A poem's not too heavy for a branch.
I'll write as many as you ask for,
as many poems
                as there are trees!
How shall we get on in the future together?
Perhaps, we shall soon forget this?
No,
        if we have trouble on the way,

we'll remember
            that somewhere,
                        bathed in light,
a tree
      is waving
            a poem,
and smiling we'll say:
                  " 'We have to go on.' " . . .

1955

TRANSLATED BY GEORGE REAVY

WHITE NIGHTS IN ARCHANGEL

The white nights—the eternal "maybe."
Something is shimmering, strangely worrying me.
Maybe it's the sun, but maybe it's the moon.
Brand new ships' officers wander about,
maybe in Archangel, maybe in Marseilles,
maybe in sadness, maybe in joy.

Waitresses, with their eyes rolling
like iceboats beneath their brows,
wander along with them arm in arm.
Can it be the roar of the nor'wester which prompts them
to stop kissing?
Maybe they should, maybe they shouldn't.

The seagulls soar crying over the masts,
maybe they're mourning, maybe they're laughing,
and at the jetty a sailor takes his leave
of a woman, with a long drawn-out kiss:
"What is your name?" "It's not important . . ."
Maybe so, maybe not.

By the jetty the thought comes to me, unbidden,
that the seagulls aren't seagulls, the waves aren't waves,
that he and she—aren't he and she.
All of that is the aurora of the white nights,
all of that is only fancy, fancy,
maybe of insomnia, maybe of a dream.

Now he's going up the gangplank onto his schooner:
"I'll bring you a sealskin!"
But he's forgotten he doesn't know where.
The woman remains standing there in silence.
Who knows—maybe he'll come back.
Maybe no, maybe yes.

The schooner gives a drawn-out hoot of farewell . . .
He doesn't look sad any more.
Now he is sailing, detached and remote,
telling dirty stories with relish
on what may be a sea, on what may be a schooner.
Maybe it's him, maybe somebody else.

And namelessly by the jetty—
maybe it's an end, maybe a beginning—
stands the woman, in a thin gray coat,
slowly melting away like a patch of mist.
Maybe she is Vera, maybe Tamara,
maybe Zoya, but maybe—no one at all . . .

TRANSLATED BY GEOFFREY DUTTON
WITH TINA TUPIKINA-GLAESSNER

LET'S NOT . . .

Let's not . . .
        Everything's ghostly—
                the blank windows
                    watching,
the snow reddening behind the stoplights of the cars.
Let's not . . .
        Everything's ghostly, lost in mist,
like a garden in March emptied of men and women,
                    paraded by
                    shadows.
Let's not . . .
        I stand by a tree,
                not speaking, undeceiving,
facing
        the double glare of the headlights,
and with a quiet hand touch
                but do not break
the tender icicle imprisoning a twig.
Let's not . . .
        I see you in the sleepy, reeling trolley
with spectral Moscow rocking in the window,
your cheek propped on a child's wool mitten,
thinking of me with a woman's rancor.
Let's not . . .
        You'll be a woman soon enough, subtle and
                    worn,
hungry for praise, for the balm of a caress;

it will be March again,

                                a callow boy will whisper in your ear,
your head will whirl inconsolably.
Let's not . . .
                 For both your sakes,
don't stroll with him down the slippery paths,
don't place
                your insubordinate hands
upon his shoulders,
                        even as I do not place them today.
Let's not . . .
                 Oh disbelieve, like me, in the ghostly city.
Be spared
             from waking in the wasteland,
                       terrified.
Say: "Let's not . . . ,"
                bending your head,
as I this moment
             say
                "Let's not . . ."
                       to you . . .

1960

TRANSLATED BY STANLEY KUNITZ
WITH ANTHONY KAHN

THE SNOW WILL BEGIN AGAIN

The snow will begin again, falling, falling,
and in its canvas I will read
the image of my youth again, calling
me wherever it may lead.

And it will lead me by the hand to the mystery
of someone's shadow, the tap of feet,
drawing me into the old, old conspiracy
of the lights, the trees, the blizzard in the street.

And those Moscow streets, the Mokhovayas,
the Stretenka, it will seem to me,
it will seem to me I still have not been young yet
but am touching the possibility.

And the vortex of night will start whirling, whirling,
and I will be funneled into wrong,
and my youth I have been following will be curtained
off by snow, nothing will belong.

But suddenly under the impartial sunstream
all her makeup is there to see,
like a gypsy bitch who has rubbed her orgasm against me
my youth will clear off and abandon me.

I will start over again, and change my life's pattern,
will put my naïveté to shame,
and gloomily will hold out my neck and attach
myself, like a stray dog, to a chain.

But the snow will begin again, falling, falling,
everything turning round like a spindle,
and my youth like a gypsy girl will be calling
again to me outside my window.

And the snow will begin again, falling, falling,
and I will gnaw my way through the chain,
and my life like a snowball will be rolling
towards a girl's fur boots again.

TRANSLATED BY GEOFFREY DUTTON
WITH IGOR MEZHAKOFF-KORIAKIN

TO MY DOG

With black muzzle pressed against a pane,
a dog keeps waiting, waiting.

I lay my hand upon its coat,
and also wait for someone to appear.

Do you remember, dog, there was a time
when a woman was living in this house?

But who was she to me?
A sister or a wife maybe,

and, at times, a daughter, too,
whom I felt obliged to help.

She's far away now . . . You're so quiet.
No other women will come here.

My dear old dog, you're good in every way,
but what a pity you don't drink.

1958

TRANSLATED BY GEORGE REAVY

LOVE'S MATURITY

Love's maturity, you say?
                              Is that so?
Straining,
          I wait.
                    You come.
Glances meet!
              No shudder, even!
Instead, repose . . .
                        as though winded by a blow.
Fingers touch!
              No explosion, even! ! !
Instead, repose . . .
                        ready to howl, I run.
Is that all
          between you and me?
Are ashes
          the maturity of fire, then?
Is love's maturity
                    no more than affinity,
and that only
          in the best of cases?
Who's playing the monster over us,
wicked and leering?
Who, with cold efficacy,
dared fabricate a false definition?
Love has its birth and death.
Love has no maturity.

Love roars,
          stoking
the menace of extinction for us,
and it breathes
              not with equanimity,
but huskily
gasps—
          begging for mercy
and no mercy—
                  as the stifling earth gasps,
abandoned by reason,
half-smothered by the world's creation . . .

1964

TRANSLATED BY GEORGE REAVY

I FELL OUT OF LOVE WITH YOU

I fell out of love with you—what a banal denouement,
just as banal as life, just as banal as death is.
Let me snap the string of this intolerable love song,
smash the guitar in two—why force a comedy!

Only the pup, shaggy little monster, cannot understand
why you and I make complex every simple thing.
As soon as I let him in, he runs to your door and scratches,
but he scratches at my door every time you let him in.

Really, you could go mad, dashing about like this.
Sentimental dog, I know you're immature,
but I refuse to become a sentimentalist.
To drag out the last act is to prolong the torture.

To be sentimental is not a weakness but a crime—
when you soften again, again promise reconciliation,
and, groaning, attempt to stage a show, yet another time,
under the insipid name of "Love's Salvation."

You should start saving love right at the beginning
from those passionate "Forevers!", those childish "Nevers!"
"Do not make promises!"—the trains were bellowing.
"Do not make promises!"—mumbled the telephone wires.

Half-cracked branches of trees and the smoke-smudged sky
were warning us, so ignorant in our conceit,
that optimism is merely untaught simplicity,
that hopes are always safer when they are not too great.

It is kinder to stay quite sober and soberly weigh the worth
of the links before putting them on—that's the creed of the
    chain,
not to promise heaven but at least to give the earth,
not to promise until death do part but at least give life
    again.

When you are in love it is kinder not to keep on saying,
    "I love you."
How hard it is later, from the same mouth, to hear it de-
    stroyed
in words that are void of truth, in sneers, gibes that mock
    you,
making the world we had thought perfect seem false and
    void.

It is better not to promise. Love is something one can't
    realize.
Why, then, lead someone into deceit as to the altar?
Of course the vision is wonderful, until it flies.
It is kinder not to love when you know love has no future.

Our poor dog keeps on whining, enough to drive us to mad-
    ness,
with his paws scratching now on your door, now on my
    door.
I no longer love you; for that I do not ask forgiveness.
I did love you; that is what I ask forgiveness for.

TRANSLATED BY GEOFFREY DUTTON
WITH IGOR MEZHAKOFF-KORIAKIN

LONELINESS (FAITHFULNESS)

How ashamed one is to go to the movies alone,
when no wife,
   no girl,
      no friend goes along,
where so short are the film shows
and waiting for them so long*
How ashamed one is—
     in that locked-in war of nerves
with couples in the lobby looking scoffingly—
to munch cake,
   blushingly,
      in a corner curve,
as if there was in it some kind of depravity! . . .
We,
 embarrassed by loneliness,
      seeking stimulation,
fling ourselves into some kind of company new,
and worthless friendship's servile obligations
to the very brink of the grave we pursue.
In various foolish cliques we enroll—
in some they just drink
     and are never disabused.
In others merely busy with glad rags and dolls,
and in the rest—
    opponents political arguments pursue,

---

* In the U.S.S.R. there are no continuous film shows—each is booked
like a theater, and the audience waits in the foyer for the previous audience
to exit.

but look carefully—
in them the same traits can be seen.
How varied are the forms of vanity!
There's this,
there's that noisy company . . .
I managed to escape from—
so many
As if I had been caught in a new kind of trap,
but, leaving behind bits of fur,
I escaped!
I escaped!
You're ahead of me,
freedom's
desert.
But who the hell needs you?
You're nice,
but you're just as disgusting
as an unloved wife, so faithful and trusting.
And you, my beloved?
How's life now?
Have you got rid of vanity's blight?
And whose are your slanting eyes now
and your shoulders, luxurious and white?
Since our last meeting—but a few years,
and yet look—
such banalities!
How base it all is,
my dear,
how base it is!
You think I'm vindictive, no doubt,
that I've grabbed a taxi and rush off to pursue,

but, if I'm rushing,
                              where shall I get out?
No matter what, I can't free myself of you!
With me, women retreat into themselves,
                                              sensing
that more and more foreign to me they grew.
I lay my head on their laps, musing,
that I don't belong to them—
                              I belong to you.

Why, not so long ago a girl I went to see—
in a plain-looking house in Sennaya Street.
I hung my coat on two wretched antlers curled.
Under a one-sided Xmas tree with pale lamps alight,
shining with her little slippers of white,
sat a woman,
                    as stern as a girl.
I was so easily permitted to visit her late,
so fully self-confident
                         was I,
that, too carried away with being up-to-date,
I brought her no flowers,
                              just wine.
But it turned out to be far more complicated!
She sat silent,
                    and two transparent teardrops—
two earrings,
                    like orphans isolated,
quivered in her rosy earlobes.
And like one sick,
                    looking so inarticulate,
her weak body hardly stirs,

said she dully:
                    "Go away.
                                        It's too late.
I see—
            you're not mine.
                                        You—
                                                    are hers. . . ."

Then another girl loved me, wild
with the habits of a child,
with icicle-eyes
                    and forelocks flying,
pale from gentleness and fear.
It was a stormy night
                    in the Crimea,
and the girl, under magnesia lightning,
"My dear one!
            My dear!"
                            She whispered tumultant,
putting her palms over my eyes.
All around, everything was painful and exultant,
the thunder
            and the sea's deaf-and-dumb cries.
Then suddenly,
                    with feminine intuition filled,
"You're not mine!
            Not mine!"
                            she wailed in distress.
Farewell, beloved!
                    Grimly,
                            faithfully,
                                        I'm yours still,

and loneliness the most faithful of all faithfulness.
Let not leave-taking snow on your glove tips
melt forever on my lips.
It's thanks to women,

                     so beautiful and faithless,
that it was all so fleetingly fated,
that their "Good-by"

                     is not "Au revoir" brief,
that in the queenly pride of their deceptiveness,
such blissful sufferings they give
and the beautiful fruits of loneliness.

1960

TRANSLATED BY HERBERT MARSHALL

A MOMENT HALF-WINTER,
HALF-FALL

That moment half-winter, half-fall,
what fortune did your little shoe divine?
It stirred the dead leaves up,
trying to work answers from the earth,
answers the earth wouldn't give at all.

Like a defenseless, little animal,
your shoe nuzzled its mouth against my shoe,
but, embarrassed and a little dead,
it, too, kept itself from a reply.
All about, the rustling rakes
gathered up the dead leaves at our feet.

The dead leaves hadn't yet been burned to ash.
Not I. I was consumed. Our song was sung
if, to the chaos of a shattered soul
we find no answer breaking in our own.
Looking for advice? What better words than these:
don't stir up dead leaves.

Nearby your child played in the sand.
Across the way, at home, so limitless his trust,
your husband, moving his fanatic brush,
did a landscape with a setting sun.
I felt like a knave. A two-face
doing off with someone else's colors.

55

As usual, the dead leaves burned and sank,
issuing their smoke in mute chorals.

A chorus of crows darkened the landscape
and branches, bearing mist in their pale arms,
the same dead leaves, same you, same empty bench
and child. Good God, like a phantom of betrayal,
will I, too, rise, uncovered by the brush?

Life had no use for my amusements.
I was greedy. This childlike hunger, unappeased,
at times transformed itself to ruthlessness
that dismissed the longed-for apple with one bite.
Omnivore, you're more than criminal
if you work another family's grief.

A crime before a brother is a crime
before mankind. It's just as much a sin
to wrong entire nations
as to do a single family in
and just as base, if you can't build another,
to bring a passing life down on the fly.

The trolley bell is a prophetic bell.
I'm on the footboard, roadways flashing by.
Alone again. No matter, it'll pass;
it's not the first time. Or the last.
Still, better isolation than, for warmth,
a bonfire of live souls, like dead leaves at my feet.
What else could I do? The tale's complete.

TRANSLATED BY ANTHONY KAHN

56

WHY ARE YOU LIKE THIS?

When the radio operator of the *Morianna,* head bent,
was searching for a radio beacon,
by chance he picked up on the receiver a woman's voice:
"Why are you like this, why are you like this?"

From Amderma* she shouted
across the masts and ice and barking dogs,
and like a storm it grew louder all around:
"Why are you like this, why are you like this?"

Pressing inhumanly against each other,
crunching on all sides against each other,
each ice floe wheezed to the other:
"Why are you like this, why are you like this?"

With all its being, the white whale
tangled in the nets cried to the hunter
through a fountain of blood:
"Why are you like this, why are you like this?"

And he, poor fellow,
swept away by a curling wave,
whispered as he perished without trace:
"Why are you like this, why are you like this?"

* Port on Kara Sea, 260 miles northeast of Archangel.

Like a swine I betray you
and nothing will stop me,
while all the time your eyes implore me:
"Why are you like this, why are you like this?"

You look at me, estranged and full of hate,
already almost like an enemy,
and hopelessly I implore you:
"Why are you like this, why are you like this?"

And heart to heart, nation to nation,
every year more distrustfully
they shout through storms and darkness:
"Why are you like this, why are you like this?"

TRANSLATED BY GEOFFREY DUTTON WITH
TINA TUPIKINA-GLAESSNER

IN AIRCRAFT

In aircraft, the newest, inexorable models,
I was zooming up like passion,
Flying from hope to hope,
Killing this one, then that one.

But hope was in the middle,
Beyond this flinging and the take-off markers,
Like a seal on a chip of ice
With its sad muzzle lifted.

I pressed my lip to my lip
On the bitter sweetness of flight
Candy, but got scared quick, bursting with a double love
Like an empty aerogram.

Tenderness called me like the void
Into the rustling of fallen-off clothes,
But the touch of any hope plunged me
Again into hopelessness.

I sped back and forth in a sick panic,
With a hard-hit mask of a face,
With a mind split two ways,
Both ways false.

Look: once, through the whirling of the earth,
I saw from a taxi window
That a center-split pine
Moaned by the road like a lyre.

So you see it wasn't *that* crazy
That, a flying Wandering Jew, I
Involved the sky—right?—I said
The sky, in my private life.

And the straight routes of the flights slice through
The downpours, now here, now there—you almost want to
    cut them,
Like the strings of a groaning lyre
Between two hopeless hopes.

TRANSLATED BY JAMES DICKEY
WITH ANTHONY KAHN

ON THE DEATH OF A DOG

Pinned by the plague,
whimpering good-by,
his eyes, a wounded brother's,
the dog wants to die.
The twisted body, shortened breath,
pray for an end, and a refuge
in death.
"I did my best to help you live,
now help me die."
In the vet's dirty sty of a temple,
to the moan of experimental
cows, he bids us good-by,
and writhes,
and rips the bed.

A man of few words, the vet
(concentration itself)
fills the syringe
with the mercy of death.
Galia leans into my shoulder.
What a bitter pill:
the only way to be of help
is to be on hand to kill.

Wherever souls migrate
the truth will out:
a coward's still a coward,
a louse remains a louse.

And so, as I hold you,
there's reason for tears:
only the best souls
reappear as dogs.
Moving their ears in the darkness,
even at Heaven's gate,
where angels may or may not await us,
our dead dogs wait.
You'll wait for me, my brother,
as sure as trust, as true,
by Heaven or Hell, like a sober mind
when the drinking's through.
And when free at last
(and secretly glad)
my soul sails home
and they lay me out
I'd rather I had
not a candle to hold
but a bone for my dog.

TRANSLATED BY ANTHONY KAHN

NO, I'LL NOT TAKE THE HALF

No, I'll not take the half of anything!
Give me the whole sky! The far-flung earth!
Seas and rivers and mountain avalanches—
All these are mine! I'll accept no less!

No, life, you cannot woo me with a part.
Let it be all or nothing! I can shoulder that!
I don't want happiness by halves,
Nor is half of sorrow what I want.

Yet there's a pillow I would share,
Where gently pressed against a cheek,
Like a helpless star, a falling star,
A ring glimmers on a finger of your hand.

1963

TRANSLATED BY GEORGE REAVY

THE INEXPRESSIBLE

I want what's inexpressible!
Impudent, I play with fire without a queen

My queen-reason is under the knight's hooves
What joy to lose to the fire!

What flaming in the uncombed night
From slender you, as from a candle!

How you've fired-up
The idea of sin!

I writhe but the cry of my flesh is bliss
The heretic is already freed by the fire

Gul'ripshi
New York Paris Madrid in flames
And someone dear to me burns in them

But if from the heretic's fire
The flame leaps to some poor bastard's roof

All the heretic burns for
Shall be forever damned to hell

For truth, when you burn down the scene
of someone nearby,
Is no longer truth but a lie.

TRANSLATED BY LAWRENCE FERLINGHETTI
WITH ANTHONY KAHN

A SPECIAL VANTAGE POINT

The garden's yellows and pinks
witnessed our parting rite;
the bread on the plate imbibed
the tender drops of the grape.

She barely said a word
while, from the branch above,
one flower from the fig tree
trailed its lilac bud.

I felt her subtle touch
and heard, as if inside:
"There's a special vantage point . . .
Here . . . Open your eyes."

I tossed my head. The tree,
decked in persimmon fruit,
wrinkled as an early widow,
listed, creaked, stood firm.

It seemed the tree would speak
to forgive me, or find fault,
when suddenly it rushed at me
and, through me, sprouted out.

A kilometer or two
from the mountain top
the sea below broke into view
upon our straining eyes.

Obliterating distance
somehow, league on league,
a tiny boat now trembled
on the rusty edge of a leaf.

Suddenly I knew
what had found us out;
love is just a point of view
and nothing more, perhaps.

She was beautiful;
her majesty in this:
there was nothing that she wished,
not even an address.

Resolving everything for me,
she left beyond recall;
but what greater request could there be
than the one not asked at all?

TRANSLATED BY ANTHONY KAHN

LIGHT DIED IN THE HALL

Light died in the hall . . . Yet while, upon the boards,
Darkness arose and played the only role,
There poured through all my veins, in icy chords,
The chill of an inaudible chorale.

I knew that there, prepared for the prologue, seen
By none, perhaps, but the wide eye of God,
Like a sliver of the darkness, like a lean
Shade among shadows, slim and alive, you stood.

I had not God's high vision, yet within,
Like the voice of God, I felt the music rise,
And I saw, not with my sight but with my skin,
As with a thousand small, concerted eyes,

And there, in the dark, in the intermittencies
Of someone's breathing, the dense transparencies
Of the incorporeal shadows, I discovered
With a wild guess, and could in rapture tell
That point, apart from paradise or hell,
Where, waiting for its flame, a candle hovered.

And you were kindled, and the light re-uttered,
And the chaos of strange blackness was no more,
And only a little golden forelock fluttered
Before me, like a wind-whipped tongue of fire.

TRANSLATED BY RICHARD WILBUR
WITH ANTHONY KAHN

INCANTATION

Think of me on spring nights
and think of me on summer nights,
think of me on autumn nights
and think of me on winter nights.
Though I'm not there, but somewhere gone,
far from your side, as if abroad,
stretch yourself on the long cool sheet,
float on your back, as in the sea,
surrendering to the soft slow wave,
with me, as with the sea, utterly alone.

I want nothing on your mind all day.
Let the day turn everything upside down,
besmudge with smoke and flood with wine,
distract you till I fade from view.
All right, think of anything by day,
but in the night—only of me alone.

Over the locomotive whistles, over
the wind, ripping the clouds to shreds,
listen to me, for pity's sake:
show me again, in the narrow room,
your eyes half-shut with ecstasy and pain,
your palms pressing your temples till they ache.

I beseech you—in the stillest stillness,
or when the rain patters on your roof,
or the snow sparks on your windowpanes,
and you lie between sleep and waking—

think of me on spring nights
and think of me on summer nights,
think of me on autumn nights
and think of me on winter nights.

1960

TRANSLATED BY STANLEY KUNITZ
WITH ANTHONY KAHN

A FEW TENDER DAYS

A few tender days:
pebbles trembling away
at the touch of our feet,
toeing the waves.
On the bloom of your cheek,
in the flow of your hand,
little islands of moles,
sweet with your scent.

We had only one night:
the surf rushed the dam,
the gale-maddened shades
tried to leap from their frames
to the deep as it raged.
Looting the shores,
the gale ripped in two
the starry world formed
by storm-scented lips.

Entangled forever
like brother and sister
or ruin and rise,
passion and fear
fuel the flames;
your arms round my back,
your teeth set in pain,
you frightened yourself
and I am to blame.

One drink is enough,
the cormorant shrieks,
the glum derrick moans,
lugging sand from the beach.
Your pillow is bare:
in that desert of sheets,
meaningfully stuck:
one fine strand of your hair.

There's a strange children's home
where love's minutes and days
like lost children cry
all day and all night.
There, ever more sad,
roaming the shades,
are a few tender days:
your children and mine.

TRANSLATED BY ANTHONY KAHN

DOING THE TWIST ON NAILS

When you throw your dancing shoes out, back over your
   shoulder,
And lose yourself, you find yourself twisting on the stage,
                      dancing,
                        dancing,
                          dancing—
let that pink boy whip you around—I can tell you:
Life doesn't dance this way—
         That way dances death.
Thighs
      shoulders
            breasts:
                   they're all in it!
Inside you, dead drunk,
             wheezes of air are dancing.
Somebody else's ring
           dances on your hand,
And your face by itself
             doesn't dance at all
Flying, lifelessly, above all the body's life
Like a mask taken off your dead head.
And this stage—
           is only one part of that cross
On which they once
          crucified Jesus;
The nails shot through to the other side, and you began

To dance on them,
                    sticking out.
                                        And you dance
On the nails
              nails
On scandals red as rust
                        on the thorn-points of tears: Listen,
Because I once loved you, tiresomely, gloomily,
I also hammered the crooks of my nails
                                        into this stage.
Ah, bestial, beastly music,
                    do you keep on getting stronger?
No one can see the blood
                        ooze from your foot-soles—
To wash the steps with clean water,
I'd rather you'd do it, Mary Magdalene,
                                        not Jesus.
I'll wash all their days, their yesterdays, not like a brother
    would
For a sister,
                but like a sister for a sister.
I'll kneel down and pick up your feet
And hold them quietly, and with kisses try to do something
About their wounds.

TRANSLATED BY JAMES DICKEY
WITH ANTHONY KAHN

BLACK AND WHITE

To Lannie MacNulty

I

Senegal,
I dive to the very dregs of the pubs
                    safe from toadies and narks,
with black circles
round my eyes
          after crazy nights of crashing around in the dark.
I spit
on all those hypocrites splashing on the surface—
                              those and these,
and I swim
amongst the underwater plants,
          the violet-shimmering bodies.
Wailing,
two mulatto girls shake on the stage
          and under them the earth thrashes.
Their gaze
is greedy as sea anemones
          inside the tentacles of their eyelashes.
But, caught through
the smoke-fumes scarce swaying
          I am drawn across years and hours
by your two
brown eyes,
          like two truthful underwater flowers.

We are bound
together, children of fated, Shakespearean feuding and
                                                    hating,
the White House
the Grey House*
we've forced our way through your nets
                    to our very own meeting.
We're on the run,
they're after us,
        with bloodhounds, sirens, bedlam's blare.
We have flung
ourselves at the feet of our one true mother—
                        eternity, stroking our hair.
Lannie—
        you've landed
beside me like a doe
            who has jumped over seas, rockets and
                                            destroyers.
Where is the banned
border zone between us?
                        Only my skin and yours.
So try
to jump over even this border
            and give me your open lips to drink right down.
If we two lie
skin pressed into skin
            we will make ourselves one.
O night,
        scream!

* Yevtushenko's note: "The Grey House" is what the progressive youth
of South Africa call their Parliament House.

76

Drunken mobs are exploding inside you
                like an atomic nightmare.
Knives gleam
and flicker like maddened fish
                over the seaweed of hair.
Scraped back,
chairs take off into the air,
                brass knuckles scrunch into guts.
Like maniacs
whites stab blacks,
                blacks whites,
                        and the yellow hack them all to bits.
Over bellowing cattle
and above the brawling,
                as if icy Biblical clouds rang,
hail rattling,
the cocktail shaker dances
                in the barman's tenacious passionless hands.
The switch-blade twists
through ribs, the cosh smashes home
                while the barman stands above the crunch of
                        bones and claws—
God exists!—
the barman whips up our souls
                into a cocktail ordered
                        centuries before.
Over thieves
over beasts
                I cautiously take hold of your white hand.
We have each other.

"Aren't you frightened?" I ask with my eyes,
          and your eyes answer: "No, I'm not frightened."
What do I care
for the malice of all the world's bandits,
                    or its coming doom,
if through the glare
          of this horrible brawl
                    a face
                         is coming to me?
What is the cause
of this brawl?
          Why should we care!
                    And maybe, all these knives
draw us
together
          to press one to the other
                    in this maelstrom of nights.
What is love?
It is you, and it is I
          over the brass knuckles, the shots,
                    the assaults on existence.
What is love?
It is the eternal OVER
          the throat-cutting of races, prejudices,
                                   systems.
What is love?
It is the eternal OUTSIDE.
It's outside all fights, all sorts of brawls,
          it's the union of Juliet and Romeo.
What is love?
"Aren't you frightened?"—the question with the eyes,
          and the eyes' answer, "No."

II

I came to see you off
            with my two dark helpless hands—
not laden with flowers.
My Irish girl, farewell for ever . . .
                        But maybe?
                              Do you understand . . . ?
Good-by, until we meet again . . .
Your name remains safe with me
                        to my last hour,
sacred,
            Lannie.
If only we could see each other in this world
                        at least once more . . .
Good-by, until we meet again!
"Ladies and gentlemen,
            the aircraft for Paris
                        ready for departure!"
On a conveyor belt
suitcases swim
            as if along a gray river to nowhere,
into the Caravelle.
We hold each other tight
            lost like savages
in the hullabaloo
            of speculators in
                  hashish,
                        ideas,
                              prostitutes,
                                    and
even us two.

We are powerless, you and I,
                and maybe we are just infantile,
and spineless?
There are handcuffs on my hands
                        and shackles on my ankles,
the only difference—
                they don't clank.
I'm giving you away
                and you are giving me away—
                        whoever may win,
we are running away.
The handcuffs on your hands
                        show through
                                your white skin
cutting their way.
We are prisoners of our age,
                prisoners of our governments and of our race.
Everywhere
        there are fetters.
Of real freedom, for you or for us,
                        there is no trace.
Only
        a few minutes,
then the python,
                having set free his collapsing victim,
claps on
        his coils again.
What is love?
                Only a minute of freedom.
                        Then
a relapse
        to worse pain.

People do not have rights
                    beyond the ancient right to suffer,
but even in this
the coils of our era
            do not offer
us this
        mean choice.
This age has squeezed our souls,
            and, teasing us with illusions of freedom,
breaks them brutally.
If he who is trapped in the coils
                    can't have aeons of freedom,
then take
        a minute!
And afterwards—
        you can hang me,
                skin me by slow degrees,—
just as you need!
But first give me the right
                to suffer as I please,
just as I please!
Let us suffer once more
            if once more I can have what you can give—
then farewell, again!
We think—does that mean we live?
            No, we suffer, that means we live,
to share hell again!

TRANSLATED BY GEOFFREY DUTTON
WITH IGOR MEZHAKOFF-KORIAKIN

MISUNDERSTANDING

Misunderstanding's everywhere the same,
In Russia,
       in Tahiti,
             in Japan:
I loved you so
          it nearly drove me mad—
and you didn't understand.
Your curiosity was satisfied,
                  things died,
you turned your heel upon my heart:
good-by, my wings, my song.
"Darling, you didn't love me!"
                    Ysenin wept the same,
and so a fact became a fairy tale,
and who's to blame?
              Perhaps it was a fiction all along.
And you,
       what did you feel?
Did feeling play at all,
or did imagined feeling for imagined flowers
play main stage and take the curtain call?
Still, I hope,
          timidly, but hope,
that you were only cruel
because the child inside you
made you strong by making others fools.

And I hope
       that if I were to cast a word your way
inexcusably mean and out of hand,
you'd be the one to say,
"I loved you,
       but you didn't understand."

TRANSLATED BY ANTHONY KAHN

THE MARK OF CAIN

In Memoriam R. Kennedy

The poor pilgrims dragged themselves wearily
along to Mecca through gray Syria,
huddled
     and doubled up
the pilgrims stumbled along—
away from delusion and ferment
to repent,
     repent,
        repent . . .
And I was standing like an impenitent sinner
On the summit of the mountain
where once upon a time
         (don't stir!)
Abel was killed by Cain.
And—of all communiqués of blood
     the most unforgettable—
the elemental voice was heard:
"Cain,
     where is your brother Abel?"
But once again the Pharisees,
the fascists
     with their vile-sweet voices:
"Why do you worry about visions that are fake?
Yes,
     with Abel maybe we should have held back.

Admittedly, there was a little mistake,
But generally speaking we were on the right track . . ."
And I was standing on the summit
between those ahead and the hosts behind,
above a world
                    where people could commit
every corruption of their own kind.
There was no lightning
                    and no thunder,
but the stones were crying with mouths opened wide:
"The corruption of the soul may be bloodless
but it is also fratricide!"
And I imagined a gloomy, dead
brick orphanage,
                    where as with henbane
the children of Abel are spoonfed
with lies by the children of Cain.
And in the faces of Abel's children,
doing what they know that they must do,
which is always to stay silent,
the red mark of Cain shows through . . .

And I, no one's murderer,
was standing
                    on the sticky summit,
but my conscience murmured
like the Bible:
                    "You won't be able to quit!
You're corrupting your spirit with lies,
and your spirit is crumbling,
                    cracking inside.

And to kill yourself
                    —you cannot disguise
that that is also fratricide!
And how many women, you twister,
lie like crucifixions along your way—
but women, they are your sisters,
worth more than brothers can repay.
And the Hussars' toasts 'To the Ladies,'
what are they worth?
                    Bravado,
                              snide.

To kill love—
                    you cannot evade it,
that is also fratricide.
And someone's gray
                    brown eyes
staring at you with disdain,
on your forehead cicatrize
you with the eternal mark of Cain . . ."
I shuddered:
                    —Quiet, O conscience.
You know this is not comparable,
it is like comparing a children's circus
with a bloody Roman shambles . . .
But the shadow of bony Cain
jutted out from the rocks near at hand,
and the blood of the brother he had slain
was endlessly dripping from my hand.
"Look—
                    my bloody hands shake.
As a child it was fun to improvise,
out of curiosity to break

86

the velvet wings of butterflies.
Everything begins with the butterflies
and then—
        fratricide!
What will you say
            to the eternal skies
and the court of stars
               when you cannot turn back—
To say I am sinless would be telling lies,
but generally speaking I'm on the right track!
You know, all those whom you hate
set this up as the true state,
while the cigarettes take on
the smell of burning flesh, the Winstons
                and the Kents,
and the bullet
        which passed through John
kills Robert Kennedy.
And the bombs charge the earth, turn
brown villages blood-red, fire-black.
Admittedly they fall on children,
but generally speaking they're on the right track . . .
Everything begins with the butterflies,
later it comes round to bombs . . .
No amount of washing purifies—
the blood on your hands will be your doom.
The only murder which is fit—
is to kill
      the Cain inside!"
And I losing my footing on the sticky summit
face to face with the infinite
tore the flesh open in my side

and the strangled
                    embryo Cain
                              died.
I was strangling everything mean and evil,
all that later you would despise,
but it was far too late to heal
the broken wings of the butterflies.
And the wind, blood-soaked, invisible,
lashed at me from the fury of space
as if the pages of the Bible
were lashing
                    me
                    on my face.

Damascus-Moscow
1967–68

TRANSLATED BY GEOFFREY DUTTON
WITH IGOR MEZHAKOFF-KORIAKIN

WAKING

Waking then was like dreaming.
Waking then was like a lonely dream
in this cottage in this settlement,
thinking: time to go and pick mushrooms,
and ruffling your hair to wake you,
and kissing your eyes open,
all this each day a new discovery.
We stayed on at the settlement for a month,
gardens, chirping birds,
the meadow paths winding among the wheat,
tense creak of the floorboards underfoot.
And when we cut the sunflower into two
there was no need for special explanations.
When under the presentiment of dawn
we ran down into the river
(gudgeon tickle your feet in those reaches)
there was no place for complicated questions.
At first it didn't seem a mystery
incapable of human explanation
that you lay dreaming in the night beside me.
I thought it due from a just destiny
that every morning was my rendezvous
with you, which never could or would be broken.
And how I flattered myself
from time to time with proving to myself
nothing in you could be unknown to me.
You don't belong to the mind's calculations,

and you disproved each of my demonstrations,
since to be unexpected is your truth.
You came to me never with what I knew,
never the days' familiar repetitions,
but new beginnings and your new surprise.
We felt no quarrel on that droning flight,
and yet there was a presence
moving around us circle by circle,
flying with us and measuring up to us.

TRANSLATED BY HERBERT MARSHALL

MY BELOVED WILL ARRIVE AT LAST

My beloved will arrive at last,
and fold me in her arms.
She will notice the least change in me,
and understand all my apprehensions.
Out of the black rain, the infernal gloom,
having forgotten to shut the taxi door,
she'll dash up the rickety steps,
all flushed with joy and longing.
Drenched, she'll burst in
                                without knocking,
and clasp my head in her hands;
and from a chair her blue fur coat
will slip blissfully to the floor . . .

1959

TRANSLATED BY GEORGE REAVY

GIRL BEATNIK

This girl comes from New York
but she does not belong.
Along the neon lights, this girl
runs away from herself.

To this girl the world seems odious—
a moralist who's been howled down.
It holds no more truths for her.
Now the "twist" alone is true.

With hair mussed and wild,
in spectacles and a coarse sweater,
on spiked heels she dances
the thinnest of negations.

Everything strikes her as false,
everything—from the Bible to the press.
The Montagues exist, and the Capulets,
but there are no Romeos and Juliets.

The trees stoop broodingly,
and rather drunkenly the moon
staggers like a beatnik sulking
along the milky avenue.

Wanders, as if from bar to bar,
wrapped in thought, unsocial,
and the city spreads underneath
in all its hardhearted beauty.

All things look hard—the roofs and walls,
and it's no accident that, over the city,
the television antennae rise
like crucifixions without Christ.

New York, 1961

TRANSLATED BY GEORGE REAVY

SMILES

At one time you had so many smiles:
astonished, rapturous, roguish smiles,
sometimes a little sad, but all the same smiles.
But now there's not left even one of your smiles.
I'll find a field where grow hundreds of smiles.
I'll bring you a handful of the loveliest smiles,
but you'll tell me that now you don't need any smiles,
that you're so tired of others' and my own smiles.
And I'm tired too of others' smiles.
And I'm tired too of my own smiles.
I have so many defensive smiles,
making-me-still-more-unsmiling smiles.
But virtually I haven't any more smiles.
You, in my life, are the last of my smiles,
a smile, on whose face there are no more smiles.

TRANSLATED BY HERBERT MARSHALL

A DOG IS SLEEPING AT MY FEET

A dog is sleeping at my feet,
the campfire burns and dances,
and warily, from the light and shade
a woman glances.
She lies on my red jacket
beneath the silver fir
and in a reverie
says, "Sing a song," to me.
I sing. She rests, enraptured,
and to herself joins in,
her hand worrying a flower,
and, on her hand, a ring.
We spent that field trip side by side;
they all said that she
was a sober-minded woman
and here she was, in love with me.
They joked—I kept my silence.
They laughed—I built a wall.
Then the lazy, balding topographer
came to pay a call.
"Things are simpler here than Moscow,
but, brother, she's the best.
Don't think because she's Boss it matters,
she's a woman, like the rest."
I was quiet, I was serious
and all my long nights through
I'd dream of an outstanding love
full of rage and fire.

Then one day I took my blanket
and lay down in the wood.
Nearby a fence she stood,
speaking to a girl friend,
speaking about me:
Cheek against the fence I listened
and, in the branches' shade,
learned that with the likes of me
games were all she played.

I wandered to the foggy shore,
I wandered through the night
and everything looked false to me
and there was nothing right.
Neither the singing in the valley
nor the cooing brook.
I lay face downward in the wormwood
and, bitterly, I cried.
But like my very own possession
from the fluid fire
a troubled vision from the coals
arises and I see:
A dog is sleeping at my feet,
the campfire burns and dances,
and warily, from the light and shade
a woman glances.

1956

TRANSLATED BY ANTHONY KAHN

THE RESTAURANT FOR TWO

Honolulu,
you loll dreamily on your back in a silver-black nowhere.
The breeze moves moons
across the waves and along your mermaidenly thighs.
Ubiquitous scintillation.
Like a savage, you adore glinting trinkets in shopwindows.
Like brooches,
great ships ride pinned in your watery hair.
In heedless brown hands
you shuffle Yanks, Japs, and cards from Down Under.
You dance,
and tiny gilded fish tinkle in your heels.
A Scots laird
in a multicolored kilt reels with you, drooling,
and lubriciously
slips his hand under somebody's skirt, not his own.
But a modest hut,
a "Restaurant à deux," on its pilings of palm
like a gnome on stilts,
has attained to the stars, a unique toy temple.
No aerial
tops its conical cap of green leaves.
Within, the walls
are woven of bamboo and mystery, and what takes place
is *hush-hush.*
A "boy," Malayan, smirking, fetches up the stairway
baked shark's fin

steeped in pineapple, golden through and through.

Two places set.

Two candles. Two conspirators. Two fugitives.

Into each other's eyes

as if into cathedrals they have fled the world's bedlam.

It's shaky in here,

it's rickety as a Chinese lantern. Maybe it's wicked.

It's false, sure.

That is to say, it's substanceless—and still, so pleasant!

The samba's throb,

the stars' murmuring, the thunder from the breakwater—
all for these two.

Gladly I would beat it to that Restaurant à deux.

I would crush

my glass of flat champagne and shout to the sourpussed
mob:

"*I am dying,*

you bore me so. I yearn for the Restaurant à deux."

Oh no, you say?

One must do this, do that, but never, never the other?

I am fed up.

I am tired to death. I want *in* to the Restaurant à deux.

Reconsider?

Struggle on, be committed? Oh, I gave it a whack—so what?

That little hut

has shown me the answer, the exit, the Restaurant à deux.

Let them judge me!

I'm off! And yet, running away . . . is cowardly stuff.

WHAT WOULD HAPPEN

IF EVERYBODY WERE TO HIDE IN A RESTAURANT À DEUX?!

That's no way out,

in an epoch of open wounds—to seek shelter from ennui
       in a gnome-home,
in the tresses and lips of another, in her knees and brow.
       A demon's whisper
impels us to flee; we cannot comprehend
       that after flight
it is even worse than before to be a galley slave.
       . . . Amid the stars,
they sit as in a dainty boat, having had their fun, at peace,
       two fugitives:
while below them, life with its dogs like a sheriff waits.
       The Malayan
daydreams at the foot of the sacrosanct stairway
       and scornfully
entertains a stir of pity for innocence so hollow.
       He observes
a half hour remains to closing time (then, scram!)
       and switches on
the birdsong tape-recorded to lend the illusion of paradise.

1967

TRANSLATED BY JOHN UPDIKE
WITH EDWARD KEENAN

FROM DESIRE TO DESIRE

I

My honeymoon was strange,
                          both a joy and a wound.
The sweetness of honey,
                the heaviness of honey,
                          in my exhausted body.
My honeymoon was bitter,
                     a crazy chase
from desire to desire,
                     with desire behind the wheel.
The fulfillment of desire
                     is often the death of desire,
and then—a desert in the body,
                     if it really doesn't matter
whose body, next to yours,
                     has also become a desert.
And two sweating cadavers lie together.
          How many times it has been this way,
                                         but—

II

for all my offenses, life
has fully paid me out with the stars of Florida,
with the childish shamelessness of your Lolita hands,
and the purity of your Cinderella eyes.
When in one's soul
                there is calculating sobriety,
then even a kiss
                is lewd and loathsome.

In love all impertinence is permitted,
shamelessness unvarnished is permitted.
Sex alone

        is no more than reciprocal masturbation.
The bed is pure

            when an angel is at your side.
The one who loves,

              God has saved from the dirt.
And we loved, however best we could.
Desire never adorned itself in words.
After fulfillment

           desire did not end.
Desire pitched and rolled in our eyes.
Desire radiated from our skin.
Desire itself desired us.

III

The love of two moving cadavers
dressed in naked words,
even with all the tricks refined,
is dead,

    dead,

        dead.
Love is alive,
the love of people, that is,

           and not brute animals—
when with desire,

        the one you desire
gazes into your eyes.

IV

Hobos in a car,
we stopped,

      and stopped,

         and stopped

and never stopped loving
with love's own permission.
Love is
        the master license
to kill dark instincts,
        the religion
of all the unfortunate,
        the party
of all the oppressed.
Through all the chewing of chewing gum,
over all America,
flew our unquenchable desire,
pure like the Virgin's body.
Deadly curves screamed,
neon hissed,
                docks creaked.
Motel Bibles whispered,
their pages turning over with our breathing.
Elegant ladies looked askance
as we embraced,
                but nonetheless,
the alligators understood us
with their kind,
                fatherly eyes.
Primary campaigns were in full swing:
hustling,
        wheeling,
                dealing,
but we had such good luck,
we simply elected each other.

V

And in the starry, dragonfly twilight
a tiny fire on the pointed little end
of a dry twig of jasmine
smoldered like a firefly
through the horror of the world.
And you were fragrant
like jasmine,
                    sweet Hanna.
The honey was bitter
                         from the immutability
that you will slip away,
                         melt,
or break like a twig
and cease to scent the air about you.
But the honey roams through me
                              in syrupy leisure,
rewarding everything,
and blinding and scalding within
a star is born again.
And at the earliest early each morning,
when the blue honey of desire is rocking,
the roar of the Gulf of Mexico
impatiently awakens us.
All problems of laundry and repair
are flooded by the honey.
                         Your freckles
move in the foreground
                         like grains of sand
fastened by the ocean,
or like spray from that honey
whose pseudonym for us is nature.

A whole day was too little for the honey.
Desire smoldered through our eyelashes
and on your breast arose
two cranberries from St. Louis.

VI

Love each other under the shower,
love each other under the shower,
love each other under the shower,
in the hour given by God,
as though you were standing under the honey,
as though you were standing under the honey,
as though you were standing under the honey,
that washes all tiredness away.

VII

When there is no love,
                    how foul
                              and disgusting
to copulate—
                    even though you sob with tears.
When we love,
                    nothing is base or tasteless.
When we love,
                    nothing is shameful.
When we love,
                    there is freedom within.
The honey liberates us
                    from bondage,
and the smell of honey,
                    and the smell of honey
forgives everything,
                    permits everything.

When we love,
                    it is not our fault
that the thirst for honey dances in our throats,
and all who love
                    are Huckleberry Finns
with mustaches of honey
                              they've snitched.

VIII

They are unhappy whose
body and soul are parted.
To make love, as one makes something,
is all that they have been given.
How boring to be a playboy.
Who was Don Juan? A castrate.
It's no purer to be a monk.
A kind of debauchery.
But we sinned boldly,
sinned without sinning.
The soul was as the body
and the body as the soul.
Eyelashes to eyelashes,
thick honey moving through them,
and there was no boundary
between the body and the soul.

IX

How happy,
                    how happy I am, Hanna,
my gray-eyed honey,
                    my light,
that the sometime arrogance in me is gone,
and the sometime cynic has disappeared.

O my soul, do not die,
and be not alien to my body.
The body can never be a desert
when filled with the soul.

X

The slow death of desire,
both mine and yours.
Slow, ductile honey, mighty honey,
give not satisfaction, give thirst,
torment me with the ebbing of the tide,
reward me with its flood.

XI

Setting the body above the soul,
                    life deserves a monster.
Setting the soul above the body
                is a false kind of freedom.
Help me, mother nature,
                not to be among the crippled.
Help me, so that the sweetness,
            so that the heaviness,
                    so that even the bitter taste
                    of honey,
will glue my soul and my body
            together forever!

TRANSLATED BY ALBERT C. TODD

THE SIGH

He's shut his mind, friend,
                        shut and barred it—
He's made himself turn wholly inward.
He's slammed the lid down,
                        like a well-top,
Upon his depths of dark despair;
His thoughts are pounding on that well-top
And beating to come out for air.
He'll tell his thoughts to no one, hides them—
Won't sob them out in tearful floods.
The pressure's building up inside him,
And I'm afraid that he'll explode.
But he does not—
                  we only hear
A sigh,
        like woman's stifled tears,
Like restless sucking as the waves
At twilight lap the rock-strewn caves.

"I once was open, frank; my pride
Was never told to hold back or flinch,
And that's why fate has flayed my hide
And savaged me—sarcastic bitch!
I've had enough.
                I've barred the door.
I do not smile now any more.
The pain inside hurts like a blow.

I feel
      I may explode
              right now,
But I do not—
            I only hear
My sigh,
         like woman's stifled tears,
Like restless sucking as the waves
At twilight lap the rock-strewn caves . . ."

"My dear old friend,
             my misanthrope,
Sit down as once we did—there's hope;
Fill up two glasses, damn the weather,
And let us sigh—
          but sigh together . . ."

TRANSLATED BY MICHAEL GLENNY

UNREQUITED LOVE

Love unrequited is a crushing yoke;
But if you see love as a game,
                                    a trophy,
Then unrequited love's absurd, a joke—
Like Cyrano de Bergerac's odd profile.

One day a hard-boiled Russian in the theatre
Said to his wife, in words that clearly hurt her:
"Why does this Cyrano upset you all?
  The fool!
                Now I, for instance, I would never
Allow some bitch to get me in a fever . . .
I'd simply find another one—
                                    that's all."

Behind his wife's reproachful eyes there gleamed
A beaten, widowed look of desperation.
From every pore her husband oozed,
                                    it seemed,
The lethal sweat of crude self-satisfaction.
How many are like him—
                                great healthy men,
Who, lacking the capacity to suffer,
Call women "chicks" or "broads";
                                    it sounds much tougher.
Yet am I not myself a bit like them?
We yawn
            and play at shabby little passions,

Discarding hearts as though they're last year's fashions,
Afraid of tragedy,
                              afraid to pay.
And you and I, no doubt, are being weaklings
Whenever we, so often, force our feelings
To take the easier,
                              less binding way.

I often hear the inner coward whining,
From murky depths my impulse undermining:
"Hey, careful now;
                              don't get involved . . ."
I weakly take the line of least resistance,
And lose, who knows, from sheer lack of persistence,
A priceless chance of unrequited love.

A man who's clever and can use his head
Can always count on a response from woman,
For poor Cyrano's chivalry's not dead:
It is not men who show it now, but women.
In love you're either chivalrous
                              or you
Don't love.
                    All men of one law stand indicted:
If you can't love with love that's unrequited,
You cannot love—no matter what you do.

God grant us grace that we may know the pain
Of fruitless longing,
                              unreturned emotion,
Delightful torment as we wait in vain:
The hapless happiness of vain devotion.

For secretly I'm longing to be brave,
To warm my ice-cold heart with passion's burning;
In lukewarm love affairs enmeshed,
                              I rave
Of unrequited love and hopeless yearning.

TRANSLATED BY MICHAEL GLENNY

THORNS OF THE STEPPELAND

Amid sun-withered thorns of the steppeland
(There was something of you in those spines),
As you opened the fingers of each hand
I saw rings on them—rings that weren't mine.

In the crackle of thorns, dry and rotten,
Were the notes of a grating refrain
As your lips spoke of loves long forgotten—
Not of mine, not of mine, not of mine.

As you reeled off your life's little history
You said much, very much, but not all:
Deep within lay an unopened mystery,
Like a hedgehog curled up in a ball.

Though you yielded to me and caressed me,
Yet your innermost self stayed apart;
While your quivering body still pressed me
There were secrets locked up in your heart.

Amid sun-withered thorns of the steppeland,
In a riot of flowers full-blown,
I tried cunning to wheedle your secrets:
In exchange I would tell you my own.

But your eyes only begged me and pleaded,
And you moved me to shame as you said:
"What is my life to you? Do you need it?
Is your own not sufficient instead?"

As if frightened of letting it creep out,
Though making an effort of will—
You revealed just the tip of a secret,
Like the moon peeping out round a hill.

TRANSLATED BY MICHAEL GLENNY

GRATITUDE

She whispered: "Yes, he's sleeping now I'm sure."
To screen her young son's crib she drew the curtain
And put the light out; fumbling and uncertain,
She shivered, dropped her bathrobe to the floor.

We did not talk of love; instead, beneath
The sheets she whispered softly to me, burring
The letter "R" as though a cat lay purring
Behind the bright, white curtain of her teeth:

"I'd written off my chances in this life;
I was a drudge, a work horse. . . . Am I dreaming?
All that has changed; you gave me back the feeling
That I'm a woman—it's beyond belief!"

Yet I'm the one who should show gratitude.
Although I played the hunter, I was hunted;
And in its yielding, grateful attitude
Her gentle body gave the peace I wanted.

She wet my cheeks with tears, she spoke my name
And lay, exhausted, as her soft limbs flanked me;
It burned me with a wave of ice-cold shame,
Because this woman felt the need to thank me.

For I should serenade her with my verse,
And, blushing and confused, surrender to her.
But that a woman thanked me! It's perverse;
And just because a man was tender to her!

How has this happened in the world today—
To so forget a woman's primal meaning
And cast her from her rightful place? I say
To make her be man's equal is demeaning.

Absurd the difference between our "now" and "then":
The day's already come (at least it's coming),
When women will almost resemble men
And men take on the character of women.

How hard beneath my fingers in that bout
Her naked shoulder thrust with all its fullness,
And how her eyes, once dim with neuter dullness,
Became a woman's eyes as she cried out!

And then in twilight dark her eyes were veiled,
Two distant candle-flames, elusive, glowing . . .
My God—how little does a woman need
For her to feel herself once more a woman!

TRANSLATED BY MICHAEL GLENNY

THE FAMILY

And she, the woman whom you loved,
       whose life you've made a hell,
Now looks at you with hate and fear
       instead of love and warmth,
As reeling home at night again
       you lean upon the bell,
And, lurching in, defile the house
       which never did you harm.

In fear, your dog will turn away,
       you kick at him and miss;
He smells the trouble that you bring
       and crawls beneath the bed.
Your little son won't come to you
       tomorrow for a kiss—
The innocence that once shone out
       from his young eyes is dead.

You wanted to assert yourself
       as prizing "freedom" more
Than ties of family and home;
       well, now that aim is won.
If you despise the family,
       it's you deserve the scorn,
If, marrying, you then reject
       your wife, your home, your son.

The thought of your unhappiness
                        is terrible; and yet
Perversely, it's a pleasure, too,
                        to justify your life
By whining to the world at large
                        that you're "misunderstood. . . ."
Just tell me: have you ever tried
                        to understand your wife?

Attack's the best defense? For shame!
                        When she who bears your name
Is so defenseless, and whose life
                        you've helped to stunt and maim;
And when remorse is just a ruse,
                        a ticket you can use
To prove repentance—and then go
                        back out and start again.

And still your son will see in you
                        the idol of his heart;
In his blue eyes the blue's so clear
                        it almost makes you stay,
Yet you forget to muss his hair
                        this time as you depart,
And loudly slamming all the doors
                        to "freedom" rush away.

Oh bless the family, dear Lord,
                        the crown of all mankind,
The very world is borne upon
                        our children's little heads;

The Holy Trinity of life
>is Father, Mother, Child.
The human race itself must be
>a family—or dead.

It's time to stop this game, you fool,
>before it is too late,
Before your wife despises you,
>before you've gone too far;
Before you are too numb to feel
>the warning hand of fate,
And still can sense the hope within
>the glimmer of a star.

TRANSLATED BY MICHAEL GLENNY

YOU WILL REMEMBER ME

In summertime you'll try
                  to think it is December;
But then the surf will call
                  from pictures on the wall.
You'll take the pictures down,
                  and still you will remember—
Just thinking of the sea
                  you will remember me.

You're working in the ward;
                  your patient drives a tanker.
But lifting the syringe,
                  you feel a sudden twinge:
Upon his freckled arm
                  you see tattooed an anchor;
At once beneath your hand
                  are fishnets, foam on sand.

You come back home from work,
                  switch on the television.
There's Cyprus on the screen,
                  a place you've never seen,
Amid Aegean waves;
                  a flash of backward vision:
The sea is the Black Sea
                  and in it you see me.

And even washtub foam,
                         the froth on orange soda,
Remind you of that sea.
                         So, trying to break free,
And wanting to forget,
                         you take a sleeping powder;
You gulp it down in haste—
                         but salt is in the taste.

Our union is sealed
                         as though by secret contract,
Whose ink is that blue sea
                         which binds your thoughts to me.
For while we are alive,
                         we'll keep a lifelong compact:
Salt sea flows through our hearts—
                         we cannot be apart.

TRANSLATED BY MICHAEL GLENNY

THE GRAVE OF A CHILD

We sailed down the Lena at evening.
The river, fast-flowing but calm,
With daughterly love and affection
Caressed the Siberian shore.
The bow wave that flared out before us
Thrilled our eyes with its pure, driven foam;
Like the surge of a chorus, insistent,
An age-old familiar song.
The thrill of illicit adventure
Set our teeth very slightly on edge,
Like the taste of fresh snow on the palate,
Like a taste of the secret of life.
The chart that the captain was holding
Was tattered and torn half across;
As it rustled he seemed to be seeing
A portent of dangers to come.
And gruffly but quietly he told us,
A frown passing over his face:
"The name of this headland we're passing
Is grim: it's 'The Grave of a Child.'"
Far older than telephone networks
Is something which links all mankind:
The long-drawn-out bond of that moment
Was snapped by a bell's urgent peal.
This world deals us no second chances;
Escapes never meet with success.
That link joining us is misfortune,

A chain that can never be cut.
I felt a sensation of choking
At the thought better not said aloud:
To link the word "child" with a gravestone
Is cruel and intolerably sad.
I thought of all those who lay buried,
Of all that lies buried in us;
Love, too, in its way, is our offspring,
And to bury that child is a sin.
Yet twice I have shoveled the earth on,
Dispatching my love to its doom.
Which one of us hasn't done likewise
And buried his love in a grave?
Without even tears of contrition—
It's become such a habit, you see—
We bury our hopes under tombstones
Like digging a grave for a child.
We are aged by accursed ambition,
By pursuit of our vain, empty goals;
There's a child that has perished within us:
Each of us is the grave of a child.
We sailed past that menacing headland,
Past grim and precipitous cliffs,
As though past a cold, naked symbol
Of loss, of unrealized hopes.
We all have been bitterly punished
For that which lies buried within;
In each one a bell is heard tolling
For ourselves and for all of mankind. . . .

TRANSLATED BY MICHAEL GLENNY

INDEX OF TRANSLATORS

INDEX OF FIRST LINES